ENOUGH

SET IN SOUL

© 2018 Tatiana Media LLC in partnership with Set In Soul LLC

Isbn: 978-0-9991770-9-9

Published by Tatiana Media LLC

All rights reserved. No part of this journal/publication may be reproduced, stored in a retrieval system, or transmitted in any form or by any means, electronic, mechanical, photocopying, recording, scanning, or otherwise, except as permitted under Section 107 or 108 of the 1976 United States Copyright Act whatsoever without express written permission from the author, except in the case of brief quotations embodied in critical articles and reviews. Please refer all pertinent questions to the publisher.

Limit of Liability/Disclaimer of Warranty: While the publisher and author have used their best efforts in preparing this book/journal, they make no representations or warranties with respect to the accuracy or completeness of the contents of this book/journal and specifically disclaim any implied warranties. The advice and strategies contained herein may not be suitable for your situation. You should consult with a professional where appropriate. Neither the publisher nor author shall be liable for any loss of profit or any other emotional, physical, spiritual and mental distress and damages, including but not limited to special, incidental, consequential, or other damages.

For general information on our other products and services, please contact our Customer Support within the United States at support@setinsoul.com.

Tatiana Media LLC as well as Set In Soul LLC publishes its books in a variety of electronic formats. Some content that appears in print may not be available in electronic books.

This Journal Belongs To

_____

Dedicated To The Star In Me.
Everyday I Shine.

TABLE OF CONTENTS

How To Use This Journal	6
About Me	8
What's Happening	9
Section One: I've Had Enough	29
Section Two: Strong Enough	172

How To Use This Journal

You are amazing. You are wonderful. You are loved. You are unique. These are things you should know about you. All of it is true. Things may not be perfect, but you are very much needed and extremely special to many. The thing about knowing this is that not everyone will be able to see your light. There are some that just choose not to see your light and don't want you to shine. So what do they do to dim your light? They pick on you. They would rather send attention your way about what you may or may not do that is not 'cool' to distract you from their own insecurities. But when you know who you are, no one will be able to change how you perceive yourself. No one can change how amazing and wonderful you are, and you don't have to stoop to their level to show them who they truly are or to get them to stop. When someone acts like a bully regardless of the number of people who support them, they are revealing how truly hurt and scared they are about what's going on within them. So you shine by just being you while they try to shine by pretending to be who they are or someone they have learned to be.

Regardless of what someone says or does to you, being picked on is never fun. It doesn't feel good. It makes you think thoughts and experience feelings you never felt. Maybe you don't know how to express those feelings. Well, this journal serves as a way to do just that. This is your private area. This is your place to truly say what you want to say without being judged. This is your space to open up and write what you can't/wouldn't say to others. This is just another place for you to shine and get past what others are saying to you and about you. Everything others are saying about you that is not lifting you up in a positive direction is a lie. This is not to be mistaken for constructive criticism. Even if what is being said about you is something that you did or even a mistake you've made, that does not define who you are and who you will be. This is a period where you will learn to grow from those who look down upon you or laugh at you because in this world the greats (regardless of their age), experience criticism. So you are not alone.

We recommend you use this journal daily. Write in this journal everyday as prompted in the morning and at night (when you feel the urge to let your feelings out). This is your place to let all your feelings and thoughts roam free. This journal is special because not everyone has one. Only the greats who are learning how to overcome a challenge possess a journal like this, and you are one of them. There are sprinkled quotes of motivation found throughout this journal to encourage you as well as freestyling sections to write and draw whatever you desire. Write down your goals and what you see for yourself in the future because that is the focus. Choose to love yourself and build towards your goals that you WILL achieve. Now let's get started.

About Me

Full Name:

Nickname:

Age:

School:

Parents:

Siblings:

I Am From:

Favorite Subject In School:

Favorite Quote:

what's Happening

What's Happening

I Started Getting Teased At The Age Of:

Who Teases Me?

Why Do They Tease Me?

I've Been Teased For (Write How Long):

To Overcome Getting Teased, I Have:

what's Happening

I Think My Teaser Is:

When Someone Calls Me Names, I Feel:

I Get Embarrassed About:

I Am Embarrassed About It Because (In Regards To The Answer Given To The Prompt Above):

I Am Known As:

What's Happening

I Have Always Felt:

I Believe:

My Best Friend Is:

My Friends Are:

People Who I Thought Were My Friends:

What's Happening

The People I Mentioned In The Previous Response, Are No Longer My Friends Because:

When I Get Angry, I Think:

When I Get Angry, I Feel:

When I Get Angry, I Want To:

When I Am Scared, I:

What's Happening

It Hurts Me When:

Everyone Thinks I Am:

I Pretend To:

I Feel Alone When:

I Like To Talk To:

what's Happening

I Have Tried To Talk To:

I Don't Like How:

When I Talk To _____,

I Feel _____.

I Wish I Could:

My Looks Make Me Feel:

what's Happening

Because I Don't Have _____,

I _____.

Because I Do Have _____,

I _____.

What I Wish Was Different:

I Would Like The Person Who Is Teasing Me To:

If I Could Be Anyone, I Would Want To Be:

What's Happening

I Like To Listen To:

I Would Like To Be:

I Don't Look Forward To:

I Look Forward To:

I Stay Focused On:

what's Happening

I Laugh At:

I Feel Safe In This Class:

I Don't Feel Safe In This Class:

It Hurts When:

The People Who Know I'm Being Bullied Are:

what's Happening

My Weakness Is:

My Strengths Are:

I Try To Fit In By:

I Wish I Can Be More Like:

I Want To Go To:

What's Happening

I Will Never Let My Bully Know:

I Feel Sorry For:

I Know I Am Going To:

In The Future, I:

I Am Awesome At:

What's Happening

I Love To:

I Do Believe:

I Don't Believe:

I Have Tried To:

Everyday I _____ To Feel Better.

What's Happening

I Can't Wait Until:

I Am Happy That:

Any New Friends I Make Will:

I Am Not Afraid Of:

What I Think Should Be Done To People Who Tease Others:

What's Happening

If I Was A Teacher, I Would:

If I Was The Bully's Parent, I Would:

If I Was The Bully's Friend, I Would:

The Bully Is Not Worth My:

When I Get Home From School/Practice, I Think About:

What's Happening

On Social Media, I Am:

On Social Media, I Feel:

On Social Media, I Get Teased About:

It's Hard For Me To Focus On:

I Will Not Allow My Bully To:

What's Happening

I Wish I Could Help My Bully:

I Know I Am:

When I Go To School, I Feel:

What Can I Do To Stop The Bullying?

Have I Ever Bullied Someone Else?

What's Happening

My Attitude Is:

I Stand Up For Myself By:

My Parents:

I Stand Up For What I Believe In By:

Why Do I Think My Bully Bullies:

What's Happening

If Someone Tried To Hurt My Friend, I Would:

I Comfort Other's Who Are Bullied By:

Am I Friends With A Bully?

I Avoid Getting Teased By:

I Think My Bully Is Hurting From:

what's Happening

I Think My Bully Became A Bully Because:

Do I Think My Bully Is Jealous Of Me?

Were My Bully And I Ever Friends?

Could My Bully And I Ever Become Friends?

Section One:

I've Had Enough

I've Had Enough

MORNING THOUGHTS:

Date: Mood:

Today I Feel: | I Look Forward To:

Today's Compliment To Myself: | I Am Happy That:

NIGHTLY THOUGHTS:

When I Saw My Bully Today I Felt:

Today I Stood Up For Myself Or Ignored My Bully By:

The Best Part Of My Day:

Who Did I Talk To About My Bully Today? _____

My Thoughts
(Write And/Or Draw Your Thoughts)

I Love Being Me.

I've Had Enough

MORNING THOUGHTS:

Date: Mood:

Today I Feel: I Look Forward To:

Today's Compliment To Myself: I Am Happy That:

NIGHTLY THOUGHTS:

When I Saw My Bully Today I Felt:

Today I Stood Up For Myself Or Ignored My Bully By:

The Best Part Of My Day:

Who Did I Talk To About My Bully Today? _____

My Thoughts
(Write And/Or Draw Your Thoughts)

10 Things No One Knows About Me....

1.

2.

3.

4.

5.

6.

7.

8.

9.

10.

I'm Okay With Those Who Don't Like Me. Not Everyone Is Meant To Recognize A Star.

I've Had Enough

MORNING THOUGHTS:

Date: Mood:

Today I Feel: I Look Forward To:

Today's Compliment To Myself: I Am Happy That:

NIGHTLY THOUGHTS:

When I Saw My Bully Today I Felt:

Today I Stood Up For Myself Or Ignored My Bully By:

The Best Part Of My Day:

Who Did I Talk To About My Bully Today? _____

My Thoughts
(Write And/Or Draw Your Thoughts)

I Am Glad That I Am Able To....

I've Had Enough

MORNING THOUGHTS:

Date: Mood:

Today I Feel: | I Look Forward To:

Today's Compliment To Myself: | I Am Happy That:

NIGHTLY THOUGHTS:

When I Saw My Bully Today I Felt:

Today I Stood Up For Myself Or Ignored My Bully By:

The Best Part Of My Day:

Who Did I Talk To About My Bully Today? _____

My Thoughts
(Write And/Or Draw Your Thoughts)

Bullying Others Is A Sign Of Weakness.

I Forgive You.

I've Had Enough

MORNING THOUGHTS:

Date: Mood:

Today I Feel: I Look Forward To:

Today's Compliment To Myself: I Am Happy That:

NIGHTLY THOUGHTS:

When I Saw My Bully Today I Felt:

Today I Stood Up For Myself Or Ignored My Bully By:

The Best Part Of My Day:

Who Did I Talk To About My Bully Today? _____

My Thoughts
(Write And/Or Draw Your Thoughts)

Other People Do Not Determine My Value And Self Worth.

I've Had Enough

MORNING THOUGHTS:

Date: Mood:

Today I Feel: I Look Forward To:

Today's Compliment To Myself: I Am Happy That:

NIGHTLY THOUGHTS:

When I Saw My Bully Today I Felt:

Today I Stood Up For Myself Or Ignored My Bully By:

The Best Part Of My Day:

Who Did I Talk To About My Bully Today? _____

My Thoughts
(Write And/Or Draw Your Thoughts)

I've Had Enough

MORNING THOUGHTS:

Date: Mood:

Today I Feel: | I Look Forward To:

Today's Compliment To Myself: | I Am Happy That:

NIGHTLY THOUGHTS:

When I Saw My Bully Today I Felt:

Today I Stood Up For Myself Or Ignored My Bully By:

The Best Part Of My Day:

Who Did I Talk To About My Bully Today? _____

My Thoughts
(Write And/Or Draw Your Thoughts)

Loyalty Means....

I've Had Enough

MORNING THOUGHTS:

Date: Mood:

Today I Feel: I Look Forward To:

Today's Compliment To Myself: I Am Happy That:

NIGHTLY THOUGHTS:

When I Saw My Bully Today I Felt:

Today I Stood Up For Myself Or Ignored My Bully By:

The Best Part Of My Day:

Who Did I Talk To About My Bully Today? _____

My Thoughts
(Write And/Or Draw Your Thoughts)

I've Had Enough

MORNING THOUGHTS:

Date: Mood:

Today I Feel: | I Look Forward To:

Today's Compliment To Myself: | I Am Happy That:

NIGHTLY THOUGHTS:

When I Saw My Bully Today I Felt:

Today I Stood Up For Myself Or Ignored My Bully By:

The Best Part Of My Day:

Who Did I Talk To About My Bully Today? _____

My Thoughts
(Write And/Or Draw Your Thoughts)

I Refuse To Entertain Critics Who Try To Hurt Me Because They Are Hurt Themselves.

I Am Capable Of Amazing Things.

I've Had Enough

MORNING THOUGHTS:

Date: Mood:

Today I Feel: I Look Forward To:

Today's Compliment To Myself: I Am Happy That:

NIGHTLY THOUGHTS:

When I Saw My Bully Today I Felt:

Today I Stood Up For Myself Or Ignored My Bully By:

The Best Part Of My Day:

Who Did I Talk To About My Bully Today? _____

My Thoughts
(Write And/Or Draw Your Thoughts)

I've Had Enough

MORNING THOUGHTS:

Date: Mood:

Today I Feel: | I Look Forward To:

Today's Compliment To Myself: | I Am Happy That:

NIGHTLY THOUGHTS:

When I Saw My Bully Today I Felt:

Today I Stood Up For Myself Or Ignored My Bully By:

The Best Part Of My Day:

Who Did I Talk To About My Bully Today? _____

My Thoughts
(Write And/Or Draw Your Thoughts)

I Wouldn't Want To Be Anyone Else.

I've Had Enough

MORNING THOUGHTS:

Date: Mood:

Today I Feel: | I Look Forward To:

Today's Compliment To Myself: | I Am Happy That:

NIGHTLY THOUGHTS:

When I Saw My Bully Today I Felt:

Today I Stood Up For Myself Or Ignored My Bully By:

The Best Part Of My Day:

Who Did I Talk To About My Bully Today? _____

My Thoughts
(Write And/Or Draw Your Thoughts)

I Am No Longer Friends With....

My Thoughts
(Write And/Or Draw Your Thoughts)

I've Had Enough

MORNING THOUGHTS:

Date: Mood:

Today I Feel: I Look Forward To:

Today's Compliment To Myself: I Am Happy That:

NIGHTLY THOUGHTS:

When I Saw My Bully Today I Felt:

Today I Stood Up For Myself Or Ignored My Bully By:

The Best Part Of My Day:

Who Did I Talk To About My Bully Today? _____

My Thoughts
(Write And/Or Draw Your Thoughts)

I've Had Enough

MORNING THOUGHTS:

Date: Mood:

Today I Feel: I Look Forward To:

Today's Compliment To Myself: I Am Happy That:

NIGHTLY THOUGHTS:

When I Saw My Bully Today I Felt:

Today I Stood Up For Myself Or Ignored My Bully By:

The Best Part Of My Day:

Who Did I Talk To About My Bully Today? _____

My Thoughts
(Write And/Or Draw Your Thoughts)

I Refuse To Feel Defeated.

Big Dreamer. Big Achiever.

I've Had Enough

MORNING THOUGHTS:

Date: Mood:

Today I Feel: I Look Forward To:

Today's Compliment To Myself: I Am Happy That:

NIGHTLY THOUGHTS:

When I Saw My Bully Today I Felt:

Today I Stoodup For Myself Or Ignored My Bully By:

The Best Part Of My Day:

Who Did I Talk To About My Bully Today? _____

My Thoughts
(Write And/Or Draw Your Thoughts)

I've Had Enough

MORNING THOUGHTS:

Date: Mood:

Today I Feel: I Look Forward To:

Today's Compliment To Myself: I Am Happy That:

NIGHTLY THOUGHTS:

When I Saw My Bully Today I Felt:

Today I Stood Up For Myself Or Ignored My Bully By:

The Best Part Of My Day:

Who Did I Talk To About My Bully Today? _____

My Thoughts
(Write And/Or Draw Your Thoughts)

I Want To Forgive....

I've Had Enough

MORNING THOUGHTS:

Date: Mood:

Today I Feel: I Look Forward To:

Today's Compliment To Myself: I Am Happy That:

NIGHTLY THOUGHTS:

When I Saw My Bully Today I Felt:

Today I Stood Up For Myself Or Ignored My Bully By:

The Best Part Of My Day:

Who Did I Talk To About My Bully Today? _____

My Thoughts
(Write And/Or Draw Your Thoughts)

I've Had Enough

MORNING THOUGHTS:

Date: Mood:

Today I Feel: I Look Forward To:

Today's Compliment To Myself: I Am Happy That:

NIGHTLY THOUGHTS:

When I Saw My Bully Today I Felt:

Today I Stood Up For Myself Or Ignored My Bully By:

The Best Part Of My Day:

Who Did I Talk To About My Bully Today? _____

My Thoughts
(Write And/Or Draw Your Thoughts)

On Today's
To-Do List:

Smile

I've Had Enough

MORNING THOUGHTS:

Date: Mood:

Today I Feel: I Look Forward To:

Today's Compliment To Myself: I Am Happy That:

NIGHTLY THOUGHTS:

When I Saw My Bully Today I Felt:

Today I Stood Up For Myself Or Ignored My Bully By:

The Best Part Of My Day:

Who Did I Talk To About My Bully Today? _____

My Thoughts
(Write And/Or Draw Your Thoughts)

I Am Good As I Am.

I've Had Enough

MORNING THOUGHTS:

Date: Mood:

Today I Feel: I Look Forward To:

Today's Compliment To Myself: I Am Happy That:

NIGHTLY THOUGHTS:

When I Saw My Bully Today I Felt:

Today I Stood Up For Myself Or Ignored My Bully By:

The Best Part Of My Day:

Who Did I Talk To About My Bully Today? _____

My Thoughts
(Write And/Or Draw Your Thoughts)

I've Had Enough

MORNING THOUGHTS:

Date: Mood:

Today I Feel: I Look Forward To:

Today's Compliment To Myself: I Am Happy That:

NIGHTLY THOUGHTS:

When I Saw My Bully Today I Felt:

Today I Stood Up For Myself Or Ignored My Bully By:

The Best Part Of My Day:

Who Did I Talk To About My Bully Today? _____

My Thoughts
(Write And/Or Draw Your Thoughts)

Being Different Is A Blessing. I Will Never Change That.

I Am Confident That Things Are Getting Better.

I've Had Enough

MORNING THOUGHTS:

Date: Mood:

Today I Feel: I Look Forward To:

Today's Compliment To Myself: I Am Happy That:

NIGHTLY THOUGHTS:

When I Saw My Bully Today I Felt:

Today I Stood Up For Myself Or Ignored My Bully By:

The Best Part Of My Day:

Who Did I Talk To About My Bully Today? _____

My Thoughts
(Write And/Or Draw Your Thoughts)

I've Had Enough

MORNING THOUGHTS:

Date: Mood:

Today I Feel: I Look Forward To:

Today's Compliment To Myself: I Am Happy That:

NIGHTLY THOUGHTS:

When I Saw My Bully Today I Felt:

Today I Stood Up For Myself Or Ignored My Bully By:

The Best Part Of My Day:

Who Did I Talk To About My Bully Today? _____

My Thoughts
(Write And/Or Draw Your Thoughts)

I've Had Enough

MORNING THOUGHTS:

Date: Mood:

Today I Feel: I Look Forward To:

Today's Compliment To Myself: I Am Happy That:

NIGHTLY THOUGHTS:

When I Saw My Bully Today I Felt:

Today I Stood Up For Myself Or Ignored My Bully By:

The Best Part Of My Day:

Who Did I Talk To About My Bully Today? _____

My Thoughts
(Write And/Or Draw Your Thoughts)

I've Had Enough

MORNING THOUGHTS:

Date: Mood:

Today I Feel: I Look Forward To:

Today's Compliment To Myself: I Am Happy That:

NIGHTLY THOUGHTS:

When I Saw My Bully Today I Felt:

Today I Stood Up For Myself Or Ignored My Bully By:

The Best Part Of My Day:

Who Did I Talk To About My Bully Today? _____

My Thoughts
(Write And/Or Draw Your Thoughts)

The Qualities Of A Good Friend....

I Know I Am A Good Friend Because....

I Can Improve On....

I've Had Enough

MORNING THOUGHTS:

Date: Mood:

Today I Feel: I Look Forward To:

Today's Compliment To Myself: I Am Happy That:

NIGHTLY THOUGHTS:

When I Saw My Bully Today I Felt:

Today I Stood Up For Myself Or Ignored My Bully By:

The Best Part Of My Day:

Who Did I Talk To About My Bully Today? _____

My Thoughts
(Write And/Or Draw Your Thoughts)

I've Had Enough

MORNING THOUGHTS:

Date: Mood:

Today I Feel: I Look Forward To:

Today's Compliment To Myself: I Am Happy That:

NIGHTLY THOUGHTS:

When I Saw My Bully Today I Felt:

Today I Stood Up For Myself Or Ignored My Bully By:

The Best Part Of My Day:

Who Did I Talk To About My Bully Today? _____

My Thoughts
(Write And/Or Draw Your Thoughts)

I've Had Enough

MORNING THOUGHTS:

Date: Mood:

Today I Feel: I Look Forward To:

Today's Compliment To Myself: I Am Happy That:

NIGHTLY THOUGHTS:

When I Saw My Bully Today I Felt:

Today I Stood Up For Myself Or Ignored My Bully By:

The Best Part Of My Day:

Who Did I Talk To About My Bully Today? _____

My Thoughts
(Write And/Or Draw Your Thoughts)

I Am Fighting To Stay The Wonderful Person That I Am Rather Than To Give In And Change To What They Want Me To Become.

I Love Who I Am, No Matter What.

I've Had Enough

MORNING THOUGHTS:

Date: Mood:

Today I Feel: I Look Forward To:

Today's Compliment To Myself: I Am Happy That:

NIGHTLY THOUGHTS:

When I Saw My Bully Today I Felt:

Today I Stood Up For Myself Or Ignored My Bully By:

The Best Part Of My Day:

Who Did I Talk To About My Bully Today? _____

My Thoughts
(Write And/Or Draw Your Thoughts)

No One Is In Any Position To Judge Me.

I Never Look Down On Others. I Look For Ways To Build Others Up.

I've Had Enough

MORNING THOUGHTS:

Date: Mood:

Today I Feel: I Look Forward To:

Today's Compliment To Myself: I Am Happy That:

NIGHTLY THOUGHTS:

When I Saw My Bully Today I Felt:

Today I Stood Up For Myself Or Ignored My Bully By:

The Best Part Of My Day:

Who Did I Talk To About My Bully Today? _____

My Thoughts
(Write And/Or Draw Your Thoughts)

I Will Never Let Anyone Stop Me From Smiling.

I've Had Enough

MORNING THOUGHTS:

Date: Mood:

Today I Feel: I Look Forward To:

Today's Compliment To Myself: I Am Happy That:

NIGHTLY THOUGHTS:

When I Saw My Bully Today I Felt:

Today I Stood Up For Myself Or Ignored My Bully By:

The Best Part Of My Day:

Who Did I Talk To About My Bully Today? _____

My Thoughts
(Write And/Or Draw Your Thoughts)

I Hold A Grudge Towards....

I've Had Enough

MORNING THOUGHTS:

Date: Mood:

Today I Feel: I Look Forward To:

Today's Compliment To Myself: I Am Happy That:

NIGHTLY THOUGHTS:

When I Saw My Bully Today I Felt:

Today I Stood Up For Myself Or Ignored My Bully By:

The Best Part Of My Day:

Who Did I Talk To About My Bully Today? _____

My Thoughts
(Write And/Or Draw Your Thoughts)

I Don't Care If Others Don't Like Me When I'm Too Busy Laughing And Having A Good Time With Those That I Am Grateful For.

I've Had Enough

MORNING THOUGHTS:

Date: Mood:

Today I Feel: | I Look Forward To:

Today's Compliment To Myself: | I Am Happy That:

NIGHTLY THOUGHTS:

When I Saw My Bully Today I Felt:

Today I Stood Up For Myself Or Ignored My Bully By:

The Best Part Of My Day:

Who Did I Talk To About My Bully Today? _____

My Thoughts
(Write And/Or Draw Your Thoughts)

I Am Bae. Bold. Amazing. Energetic.

I've Had Enough

MORNING THOUGHTS:

Date:					Mood:

Today I Feel:				I Look Forward To:

Today's Compliment To Myself:		I Am Happy That:

NIGHTLY THOUGHTS:

When I Saw My Bully Today I Felt:

Today I Stood Up For Myself Or Ignored My Bully By:

The Best Part Of My Day:

Who Did I Talk To About My Bully Today? _____

My Thoughts
(Write And/Or Draw Your Thoughts)

I've Had Enough

MORNING THOUGHTS:

Date: Mood:

Today I Feel: I Look Forward To:

Today's Compliment To Myself: I Am Happy That:

NIGHTLY THOUGHTS:

When I Saw My Bully Today I Felt:

Today I Stood Up For Myself Or Ignored My Bully By:

The Best Part Of My Day:

Who Did I Talk To About My Bully Today? _____

My Thoughts
(Write And/Or Draw Your Thoughts)

I've Had Enough

MORNING THOUGHTS:

Date: Mood:

Today I Feel: I Look Forward To:

Today's Compliment To Myself: I Am Happy That:

NIGHTLY THOUGHTS:

When I Saw My Bully Today I Felt:

Today I Stood Up For Myself Or Ignored My Bully By:

The Best Part Of My Day:

Who Did I Talk To About My Bully Today? _____

My Thoughts
(Write And/Or Draw Your Thoughts)

Names People Call Me....

Names I Call Myself....

Names I Answer To....

I've Had Enough

MORNING THOUGHTS:

Date: Mood:

Today I Feel: | I Look Forward To:

Today's Compliment To Myself: | I Am Happy That:

NIGHTLY THOUGHTS:

When I Saw My Bully Today I Felt:

Today I Stood Up For Myself Or Ignored My Bully By:

The Best Part Of My Day:

Who Did I Talk To About My Bully Today? _____

My Thoughts
(Write And/Or Draw Your Thoughts)

I've Had Enough

MORNING THOUGHTS:

Date: Mood:

Today I Feel: I Look Forward To:

Today's Compliment To Myself: I Am Happy That:

NIGHTLY THOUGHTS:

When I Saw My Bully Today I Felt:

Today I Stood Up For Myself Or Ignored My Bully By:

The Best Part Of My Day:

Who Did I Talk To About My Bully Today? _____

My Thoughts
(Write And/Or Draw Your Thoughts)

I've Had Enough

MORNING THOUGHTS:

Date: Mood:

Today I Feel: | I Look Forward To:

Today's Compliment To Myself: | I Am Happy That:

NIGHTLY THOUGHTS:

When I Saw My Bully Today I Felt:

Today I Stood Up For Myself Or Ignored My Bully By:

The Best Part Of My Day:

Who Did I Talk To About My Bully Today? _____

My Thoughts
(Write And/Or Draw Your Thoughts)

I Am My Own Hero.

I've Had Enough

MORNING THOUGHTS:

Date:　　　　　　　　　　　　　　Mood:

　Today I Feel:　　　　　　　　　　│　I Look Forward To:

　Today's Compliment To Myself:　│　I Am Happy That:

NIGHTLY THOUGHTS:

When I Saw My Bully Today I Felt:

Today I Stood Up For Myself Or Ignored My Bully By:

The Best Part Of My Day:

Who Did I Talk To About My Bully Today? _____

My Thoughts
(Write And/Or Draw Your Thoughts)

I've Had Enough

MORNING THOUGHTS:

Date: Mood:

Today I Feel: I Look Forward To:

Today's Compliment To Myself: I Am Happy That:

NIGHTLY THOUGHTS:

When I Saw My Bully Today I Felt:

Today I Stood Up For Myself Or Ignored My Bully By:

The Best Part Of My Day:

Who Did I Talk To About My Bully Today? _____

My Thoughts
(Write And/Or Draw Your Thoughts)

I've Had Enough

MORNING THOUGHTS:

Date: Mood:

Today I Feel: I Look Forward To:

Today's Compliment To Myself: I Am Happy That:

NIGHTLY THOUGHTS:

When I Saw My Bully Today I Felt:

Today I Stood Up For Myself Or Ignored My Bully By:

The Best Part Of My Day:

Who Did I Talk To About My Bully Today? _____

My Thoughts
(Write And/Or Draw Your Thoughts)

I've Had Enough

MORNING THOUGHTS:

Date: Mood:

Today I Feel: | I Look Forward To:

Today's Compliment To Myself: | I Am Happy That:

NIGHTLY THOUGHTS:

When I Saw My Bully Today I Felt:

Today I Stood Up For Myself Or Ignored My Bully By:

The Best Part Of My Day:

Who Did I Talk To About My Bully Today? _____

My Thoughts
(Write And/Or Draw Your Thoughts)

Today I Choose To Be Happy!!

I've Had Enough

MORNING THOUGHTS:

Date: Mood:

Today I Feel: I Look Forward To:

Today's Compliment To Myself: I Am Happy That:

NIGHTLY THOUGHTS:

When I Saw My Bully Today I Felt:

Today I Stood Up For Myself Or Ignored My Bully By:

The Best Part Of My Day:

Who Did I Talk To About My Bully Today? _____

My Thoughts
(Write And/Or Draw Your Thoughts)

What I Would Like To Tell My Bully....

I've Had Enough

MORNING THOUGHTS:

Date: Mood:

Today I Feel: I Look Forward To:

Today's Compliment To Myself: I Am Happy That:

NIGHTLY THOUGHTS:

When I Saw My Bully Today I Felt:

Today I Stood Up For Myself Or Ignored My Bully By:

The Best Part Of My Day:

Who Did I Talk To About My Bully Today? _____

My Thoughts
(Write And/Or Draw Your Thoughts)

I've Had Enough

MORNING THOUGHTS:

Date: Mood:

Today I Feel: I Look Forward To:

Today's Compliment To Myself: I Am Happy That:

NIGHTLY THOUGHTS:

When I Saw My Bully Today I Felt:

Today I Stood Up For Myself Or Ignored My Bully By:

The Best Part Of My Day:

Who Did I Talk To About My Bully Today? _____

My Thoughts
(Write And/Or Draw Your Thoughts)

I Believe In Myself.

I've Had Enough

MORNING THOUGHTS:

Date: Mood:

Today I Feel: I Look Forward To:

Today's Compliment To Myself: I Am Happy That:

NIGHTLY THOUGHTS:

When I Saw My Bully Today I Felt:

Today I Stood Up For Myself Or Ignored My Bully By:

The Best Part Of My Day:

Who Did I Talk To About My Bully Today? _____

My Thoughts
(Write And/Or Draw Your Thoughts)

I've Had Enough

MORNING THOUGHTS:

Date: Mood:

Today I Feel: I Look Forward To:

Today's Compliment To Myself: I Am Happy That:

NIGHTLY THOUGHTS:

When I Saw My Bully Today I Felt:

Today I Stood Up For Myself Or Ignored My Bully By:

The Best Part Of My Day:

Who Did I Talk To About My Bully Today? _____

My Thoughts
(Write And/Or Draw Your Thoughts)

I've Had Enough

MORNING THOUGHTS:

Date: Mood:

Today I Feel: | I Look Forward To:

Today's Compliment To Myself: | I Am Happy That:

NIGHTLY THOUGHTS:

When I Saw My Bully Today I Felt:

Today I Stood Up For Myself Or Ignored My Bully By:

The Best Part Of My Day:

Who Did I Talk To About My Bully Today? _____

My Thoughts
(Write And/Or Draw Your Thoughts)

What Would I Like My Bully To Tell Me?

I've Had Enough

MORNING THOUGHTS:

Date: Mood:

Today I Feel: I Look Forward To:

Today's Compliment To Myself: I Am Happy That:

NIGHTLY THOUGHTS:

When I Saw My Bully Today I Felt:

Today I Stood Up For Myself Or Ignored My Bully By:

The Best Part Of My Day:

Who Did I Talk To About My Bully Today? _____

My Thoughts
(Write And/Or Draw Your Thoughts)

I'm Always Good Enough.

I've Had Enough

MORNING THOUGHTS:

Date: Mood:

Today I Feel: | I Look Forward To:

Today's Compliment To Myself: | I Am Happy That:

NIGHTLY THOUGHTS:

When I Saw My Bully Today I Felt:

Today I Stood Up For Myself Or Ignored My Bully By:

The Best Part Of My Day:

Who Did I Talk To About My Bully Today? _____

My Thoughts
(Write And/Or Draw Your Thoughts)

Section Two:
Strong Enough

Strong Enough

MORNING THOUGHTS:

Date: Mood:

I Woke Up Thinking:

Today I Want To:

I Will:

NIGHTLY THOUGHTS:

I Know I Am: | Everyday I Get Better At:

Today I Laughed At: | My Bully No Longer Affects:

Who Did I Talk To About My Bully Today? _____

My Thoughts
(Write And/Or Draw Your Thoughts)

Strong Enough

MORNING THOUGHTS:

Date: Mood:

I Woke Up Thinking:

Today I Want To:

I Will:

NIGHTLY THOUGHTS:

I Know I Am: Everyday I Get Better At:

Today I Laughed At: My Bully No Longer Affects:

Who Did I Talk To About My Bully Today? _____

My Thoughts
(Write And/Or Draw Your Thoughts)

I'd Rather Be Loved For Who I Am Then To Pretend To Be Loved Or Respected For Hurting Others.

The Types Of Friends That I Would Like To Have Around Me....

Strong Enough

MORNING THOUGHTS:

Date: Mood:

I Woke Up Thinking:

Today I Want To:

I Will:

NIGHTLY THOUGHTS:

I Know I Am: Everyday I Get Better At:

Today I Laughed At: My Bully No Longer Affects:

Who Did I Talk To About My Bully Today? _____

My Thoughts
(Write And/Or Draw Your Thoughts)

Strong Enough

MORNING THOUGHTS:

Date: Mood:

I Woke Up Thinking:

Today I Want To:

I Will:

NIGHTLY THOUGHTS:

I Know I Am:	Everyday I Get Better At:
Today I Laughed At:	My Bully No Longer Affects:

Who Did I Talk To About My Bully Today? _____

My Thoughts
(Write And/Or Draw Your Thoughts)

Strong Enough

MORNING THOUGHTS:

Date: Mood:

I Woke Up Thinking:

Today I Want To:

I Will:

NIGHTLY THOUGHTS:

I Know I Am: | Everyday I Get Better At:

Today I Laughed At: | My Bully No Longer Affects:

Who Did I Talk To About My Bully Today? _____

My Thoughts
(Write And/Or Draw Your Thoughts)

Next Year At This Time, I Will Be....

Strong Enough

MORNING THOUGHTS:

Date: Mood:

I Woke Up Thinking:

Today I Want To:

I Will:

NIGHTLY THOUGHTS:

I Know I Am:	Everyday I Get Better At:
Today I Laughed At:	My Bully No Longer Affects:

Who Did I Talk To About My Bully Today? _____

My Thoughts
(Write And/Or Draw Your Thoughts)

Strong Enough

MORNING THOUGHTS:

Date: Mood:

I Woke Up Thinking:

Today I Want To:

I Will:

NIGHTLY THOUGHTS:

I Know I Am: Everyday I Get Better At:

Today I Laughed At: My Bully No Longer Affects:

Who Did I Talk To About My Bully Today? _____

My Thoughts
(Write And/Or Draw Your Thoughts)

I Feel Bad For The Person Who Carries That Much Hate In Their Heart To Hurt Others.

I Love Spreading Love Because Receiving It Means Everything To Me.

Strong Enough

MORNING THOUGHTS:

Date: Mood:

I Woke Up Thinking:

Today I Want To:

I Will:

NIGHTLY THOUGHTS:

I Know I Am:	Everyday I Get Better At:
Today I Laughed At:	My Bully No Longer Affects:

Who Did I Talk To About My Bully Today? _____

My Thoughts
(Write And/Or Draw Your Thoughts)

I Make Others Happy By....

Strong Enough

MORNING THOUGHTS:

Date: Mood:

I Woke Up Thinking:

Today I Want To:

I Will:

NIGHTLY THOUGHTS:

I Know I Am:	Everyday I Get Better At:
Today I Laughed At:	My Bully No Longer Affects:

Who Did I Talk To About My Bully Today? _____

My Thoughts
(Write And/Or Draw Your Thoughts)

Strong Enough

MORNING THOUGHTS:

Date: Mood:

I Woke Up Thinking:

Today I Want To:

I Will:

NIGHTLY THOUGHTS:

I Know I Am: Everyday I Get Better At:

Today I Laughed At: My Bully No Longer Affects:

Who Did I Talk To About My Bully Today? _____

My Thoughts
(Write And/Or Draw Your Thoughts)

A Letter To My Future Self....

Strong Enough

MORNING THOUGHTS:

Date: Mood:

I Woke Up Thinking:

Today I Want To:

I Will:

NIGHTLY THOUGHTS:

I Know I Am: Everyday I Get Better At:

Today I Laughed At: My Bully No Longer Affects:

Who Did I Talk To About My Bully Today? _____

My Thoughts
(Write And/Or Draw Your Thoughts)

They Want To Build Me Up To Break Me Down. I Won't Allow Them To Do That.

Strong Enough

MORNING THOUGHTS:

Date: Mood:

I Woke Up Thinking:

Today I Want To:

I Will:

NIGHTLY THOUGHTS:

I Know I Am: Everyday I Get Better At:

Today I Laughed At: My Bully No Longer Affects:

Who Did I Talk To About My Bully Today? _____

My Thoughts
(Write And/Or Draw Your Thoughts)

Strong Enough

MORNING THOUGHTS:

Date: Mood:

I Woke Up Thinking:

Today I Want To:

I Will:

NIGHTLY THOUGHTS:

I Know I Am:	Everyday I Get Better At:
Today I Laughed At:	My Bully No Longer Affects:

Who Did I Talk To About My Bully Today? _____

My Thoughts
(Write And/Or Draw Your Thoughts)

My Current Top Five Favorite Songs....

1.

2.

3.

4.

5.

Strong Enough

MORNING THOUGHTS:

Date: Mood:

I Woke Up Thinking:

Today I Want To:

I Will:

NIGHTLY THOUGHTS:

I Know I Am: Everyday I Get Better At:

Today I Laughed At: My Bully No Longer Affects:

Who Did I Talk To About My Bully Today? _____

My Thoughts
(Write And/Or Draw Your Thoughts)

Strong Enough

MORNING THOUGHTS:

Date: Mood:

I Woke Up Thinking:

Today I Want To:

I Will:

NIGHTLY THOUGHTS:

I Know I Am: Everyday I Get Better At:

Today I Laughed At: My Bully No Longer Affects:

Who Did I Talk To About My Bully Today? _____

My Thoughts
(Write And/Or Draw Your Thoughts)

I Don't Care What Other People Say About Me. I Only Care About What I Believe About Myself.

They Don't Know How To Handle A Diamond, That's Why They Treat Me As An Imitation.

Strong Enough

MORNING THOUGHTS:

Date: Mood:

I Woke Up Thinking:

Today I Want To:

I Will:

NIGHTLY THOUGHTS:

I Know I Am: Everyday I Get Better At:

Today I Laughed At: My Bully No Longer Affects:

Who Did I Talk To About My Bully Today? _____

My Thoughts
(Write And/Or Draw Your Thoughts)

Strong Enough

MORNING THOUGHTS:

Date: Mood:

I Woke Up Thinking:

Today I Want To:

I Will:

NIGHTLY THOUGHTS:

I Know I Am:	Everyday I Get Better At:
Today I Laughed At:	My Bully No Longer Affects:

Who Did I Talk To About My Bully Today? _____

My Thoughts
(Write And/Or Draw Your Thoughts)

Dear _____,

Today You Will Shine.

Strong Enough

MORNING THOUGHTS:

Date: Mood:

I Woke Up Thinking:

Today I Want To:

I Will:

NIGHTLY THOUGHTS:

I Know I Am: Everyday I Get Better At:

Today I Laughed At: My Bully No Longer Affects:

Who Did I Talk To About My Bully Today? _____

My Thoughts
(Write And/Or Draw Your Thoughts)

I Can't Wait Until....

Strong Enough

MORNING THOUGHTS:

Date: Mood:

I Woke Up Thinking:

Today I Want To:

I Will:

NIGHTLY THOUGHTS:

I Know I Am: Everyday I Get Better At:

Today I Laughed At: My Bully No Longer Affects:

Who Did I Talk To About My Bully Today? _____

My Thoughts
(Write And/Or Draw Your Thoughts)

Strong Enough

MORNING THOUGHTS:

Date: Mood:

I Woke Up Thinking:

Today I Want To:

I Will:

NIGHTLY THOUGHTS:

I Know I Am: Everyday I Get Better At:

Today I Laughed At: My Bully No Longer Affects:

Who Did I Talk To About My Bully Today? _____

My Thoughts
(Write And/Or Draw Your Thoughts)

Strong Enough

MORNING THOUGHTS:

Date: Mood:

I Woke Up Thinking:

Today I Want To:

I Will:

NIGHTLY THOUGHTS:

I Know I Am:	Everyday I Get Better At:
Today I Laughed At:	My Bully No Longer Affects:

Who Did I Talk To About My Bully Today? _____

My Thoughts
(Write And/Or Draw Your Thoughts)

They Want To Be Lovable Just Like Me.

Strong Enough

MORNING THOUGHTS:

Date: Mood:

I Woke Up Thinking:

Today I Want To:

I Will:

NIGHTLY THOUGHTS:

I Know I Am: Everyday I Get Better At:

Today I Laughed At: My Bully No Longer Affects:

Who Did I Talk To About My Bully Today? _____

My Thoughts
(Write And/Or Draw Your Thoughts)

Strong Enough

MORNING THOUGHTS:

Date: Mood:

I Woke Up Thinking:

Today I Want To:

I Will:

NIGHTLY THOUGHTS:

I Know I Am: Everyday I Get Better At:

Today I Laughed At: My Bully No Longer Affects:

Who Did I Talk To About My Bully Today? _____

My Thoughts
(Write And/Or Draw Your Thoughts)

Strong Enough

MORNING THOUGHTS:

Date: Mood:

I Woke Up Thinking:

Today I Want To:

I Will:

NIGHTLY THOUGHTS:

I Know I Am: Everyday I Get Better At:

Today I Laughed At: My Bully No Longer Affects:

Who Did I Talk To About My Bully Today? _____

Strong Enough

MORNING THOUGHTS:

Date: Mood:

I Woke Up Thinking:

Today I Want To:

I Will:

NIGHTLY THOUGHTS:

I Know I Am:	Everyday I Get Better At:
Today I Laughed At:	My Bully No Longer Affects:

Who Did I Talk To About My Bully Today? _____

My Thoughts
(Write And/Or Draw Your Thoughts)

Through The Experience Of Being Teased, I Have Learned....

Strong Enough

MORNING THOUGHTS:

Date: Mood:

I Woke Up Thinking:

Today I Want To:

I Will:

NIGHTLY THOUGHTS:

I Know I Am: | Everyday I Get Better At:

Today I Laughed At: | My Bully No Longer Affects:

Who Did I Talk To About My Bully Today? _____

My Thoughts
(Write And/Or Draw Your Thoughts)

I Choose To Focus On What's Good.

Strong Enough

MORNING THOUGHTS:

Date: Mood:

I Woke Up Thinking:

Today I Want To:

I Will:

NIGHTLY THOUGHTS:

I Know I Am:	Everyday I Get Better At:
Today I Laughed At:	My Bully No Longer Affects:

Who Did I Talk To About My Bully Today? _____

My Thoughts
(Write And/Or Draw Your Thoughts)

Strong Enough

MORNING THOUGHTS:

Date: Mood:

I Woke Up Thinking:

Today I Want To:

I Will:

NIGHTLY THOUGHTS:

I Know I Am: Everyday I Get Better At:

Today I Laughed At: My Bully No Longer Affects:

Who Did I Talk To About My Bully Today? _____

My Thoughts
(Write And/Or Draw Your Thoughts)

Ten Years From Now, I Would Like To Tell My Bully....

Strong Enough

MORNING THOUGHTS:

Date: Mood:

I Woke Up Thinking:

Today I Want To:

I Will:

NIGHTLY THOUGHTS:

I Know I Am: Everyday I Get Better At:

Today I Laughed At: My Bully No Longer Affects:

Who Did I Talk To About My Bully Today? _____

My Thoughts
(Write And/Or Draw Your Thoughts)

I Will Make A Positive Difference In This World.

My Bully No Longer Affects Me.

Strong Enough

MORNING THOUGHTS:

Date: Mood:

I Woke Up Thinking:

Today I Want To:

I Will:

NIGHTLY THOUGHTS:

I Know I Am: | Everyday I Get Better At:

Today I Laughed At: | My Bully No Longer Affects:

Who Did I Talk To About My Bully Today? _____

My Thoughts
(Write And/Or Draw Your Thoughts)

Strong Enough

MORNING THOUGHTS:

Date: Mood:

I Woke Up Thinking:

Today I Want To:

I Will:

NIGHTLY THOUGHTS:

I Know I Am: Everyday I Get Better At:

Today I Laughed At: My Bully No Longer Affects:

Who Did I Talk To About My Bully Today? _____

My Thoughts
(Write And/Or Draw Your Thoughts)

If We Can't Get Along, I'd Rather Hang Out With Those Who Love Me.

If My Feelings Could Talk, They Would Say....

Strong Enough

MORNING THOUGHTS:

Date: Mood:

I Woke Up Thinking:

Today I Want To:

I Will:

NIGHTLY THOUGHTS:

I Know I Am: | Everyday I Get Better At:

Today I Laughed At: | My Bully No Longer Affects:

Who Did I Talk To About My Bully Today? _____

My Thoughts
(Write And/Or Draw Your Thoughts)

Strong Enough

MORNING THOUGHTS:

Date: Mood:

I Woke Up Thinking:

Today I Want To:

I Will:

NIGHTLY THOUGHTS:

I Know I Am: Everyday I Get Better At:

Today I Laughed At: My Bully No Longer Affects:

Who Did I Talk To About My Bully Today? _____

My Thoughts
(Write And/Or Draw Your Thoughts)

Strong Enough

MORNING THOUGHTS:

Date: Mood:

I Woke Up Thinking:

Today I Want To:

I Will:

NIGHTLY THOUGHTS:

I Know I Am:	Everyday I Get Better At:
Today I Laughed At:	My Bully No Longer Affects:

Who Did I Talk To About My Bully Today? _____

My Thoughts
(Write And/Or Draw Your Thoughts)

Love

Laugh

Smile

Better Days. Better Future. Better Life.

Strong Enough

MORNING THOUGHTS:

Date: Mood:

I Woke Up Thinking:

Today I Want To:

I Will:

NIGHTLY THOUGHTS:

I Know I Am: Everyday I Get Better At:

Today I Laughed At: My Bully No Longer Affects:

Who Did I Talk To About My Bully Today? _____

My Thoughts
(Write And/Or Draw Your Thoughts)

Strong Enough

MORNING THOUGHTS:

Date: Mood:

I Woke Up Thinking:

Today I Want To:

I Will:

NIGHTLY THOUGHTS:

I Know I Am:	Everyday I Get Better At:
Today I Laughed At:	My Bully No Longer Affects:

Who Did I Talk To About My Bully Today? _____

My Thoughts
(Write And/Or Draw Your Thoughts)

I Will Accomplish All Of My Goals Because I Believe In Myself.

My Confidence Is Phenomenal.

Strong Enough

MORNING THOUGHTS:

Date: Mood:

I Woke Up Thinking:

Today I Want To:

I Will:

NIGHTLY THOUGHTS:

I Know I Am: Everyday I Get Better At:

Today I Laughed At: My Bully No Longer Affects:

Who Did I Talk To About My Bully Today? _____

My Thoughts
(Write And/Or Draw Your Thoughts)

Strong Enough

MORNING THOUGHTS:

Date: Mood:

I Woke Up Thinking:

Today I Want To:

I Will:

NIGHTLY THOUGHTS:

I Know I Am: Everyday I Get Better At:

Today I Laughed At: My Bully No Longer Affects:

Who Did I Talk To About My Bully Today? _____

My Thoughts
(Write And/Or Draw Your Thoughts)

I'll Be Fine Even If They Don't Like Me.

What I Will Say To Anyone Who Chooses To Tease Me In The Future....

Strong Enough

MORNING THOUGHTS:

Date: Mood:

I Woke Up Thinking:

Today I Want To:

I Will:

NIGHTLY THOUGHTS:

I Know I Am:	Everyday I Get Better At:
Today I Laughed At:	My Bully No Longer Affects:

Who Did I Talk To About My Bully Today? _____

My Thoughts
(Write And/Or Draw Your Thoughts)

Strong Enough

MORNING THOUGHTS:

Date: Mood:

I Woke Up Thinking:

Today I Want To:

I Will:

NIGHTLY THOUGHTS:

I Know I Am: Everyday I Get Better At:

Today I Laughed At: My Bully No Longer Affects:

Who Did I Talk To About My Bully Today? _____

My Thoughts
(Write And/Or Draw Your Thoughts)

Regardless Of What Is Happening, I Will Be There For Myself. I Am My Own Best Friend.

Strong Enough

MORNING THOUGHTS:

Date: Mood:

I Woke Up Thinking:

Today I Want To:

I Will:

NIGHTLY THOUGHTS:

I Know I Am:	Everyday I Get Better At:
Today I Laughed At:	My Bully No Longer Affects:

Who Did I Talk To About My Bully Today? _____

My Thoughts
(Write And/Or Draw Your Thoughts)

I Refuse To Let Hurt People Steal My Happiness.

Strong Enough

MORNING THOUGHTS:

Date: Mood:

I Woke Up Thinking:

Today I Want To:

I Will:

NIGHTLY THOUGHTS:

I Know I Am:	Everyday I Get Better At:
Today I Laughed At:	My Bully No Longer Affects:

Who Did I Talk To About My Bully Today? _____

My Thoughts
(Write And/Or Draw Your Thoughts)

Strong Enough

MORNING THOUGHTS:

Date: Mood:

I Woke Up Thinking:

Today I Want To:

I Will:

NIGHTLY THOUGHTS:

I Know I Am: Everyday I Get Better At:

Today I Laughed At: My Bully No Longer Affects:

Who Did I Talk To About My Bully Today? _____

My Thoughts
(Write And/Or Draw Your Thoughts)

There Is Nothing I Need To Be More Or Less Of. I Am Good Just Being Me.

Strong Enough

MORNING THOUGHTS:

Date: Mood:

I Woke Up Thinking:

Today I Want To:

I Will:

NIGHTLY THOUGHTS:

I Know I Am:	Everyday I Get Better At:
Today I Laughed At:	My Bully No Longer Affects:

Who Did I Talk To About My Bully Today? _____

My Thoughts
(Write And/Or Draw Your Thoughts)

It Is Not Easy To....

Strong Enough

MORNING THOUGHTS:

Date: Mood:

I Woke Up Thinking:

Today I Want To:

I Will:

NIGHTLY THOUGHTS:

I Know I Am: Everyday I Get Better At:

Today I Laughed At: My Bully No Longer Affects:

Who Did I Talk To About My Bully Today? _____

My Thoughts
(Write And/Or Draw Your Thoughts)

Strong Enough

MORNING THOUGHTS:

Date: Mood:

I Woke Up Thinking:

Today I Want To:

I Will:

NIGHTLY THOUGHTS:

I Know I Am: Everyday I Get Better At:

Today I Laughed At: My Bully No Longer Affects:

Who Did I Talk To About My Bully Today? _____

My Thoughts
(Write And/Or Draw Your Thoughts)

I Am Growing Through What I Am Going Through.

I Believe My Bully Needs....

Strong Enough

MORNING THOUGHTS:

Date: Mood:

I Woke Up Thinking:

Today I Want To:

I Will:

NIGHTLY THOUGHTS:

I Know I Am: Everyday I Get Better At:

Today I Laughed At: My Bully No Longer Affects:

Who Did I Talk To About My Bully Today? _____

My Thoughts
(Write And/Or Draw Your Thoughts)

Strong Enough

MORNING THOUGHTS:

Date: Mood:

I Woke Up Thinking:

Today I Want To:

I Will:

NIGHTLY THOUGHTS:

I Know I Am: Everyday I Get Better At:

Today I Laughed At: My Bully No Longer Affects:

Who Did I Talk To About My Bully Today? _____

My Thoughts
(Write And/Or Draw Your Thoughts)

Strong Enough

MORNING THOUGHTS:

Date: Mood:

I Woke Up Thinking:

Today I Want To:

I Will:

NIGHTLY THOUGHTS:

I Know I Am: Everyday I Get Better At:

Today I Laughed At: My Bully No Longer Affects:

Who Did I Talk To About My Bully Today? _____

My Thoughts
(Write And/Or Draw Your Thoughts)

I Was Always Meant To Stand Out And Be Myself.

Strong Enough

MORNING THOUGHTS:

Date: Mood:

I Woke Up Thinking:

Today I Want To:

I Will:

NIGHTLY THOUGHTS:

I Know I Am: Everyday I Get Better At:

Today I Laughed At: My Bully No Longer Affects:

Who Did I Talk To About My Bully Today? _____

My Thoughts
(Write And/Or Draw Your Thoughts)

I Choose To Side With Those Who Stand Against Bullying.

I Get Offended When....

Strong Enough

MORNING THOUGHTS:

Date: Mood:

I Woke Up Thinking:

Today I Want To:

I Will:

NIGHTLY THOUGHTS:

I Know I Am:	Everyday I Get Better At:
Today I Laughed At:	My Bully No Longer Affects:

Who Did I Talk To About My Bully Today? _____

My Thoughts
(Write And/Or Draw Your Thoughts)

Strong Enough

MORNING THOUGHTS:

Date: Mood:

I Woke Up Thinking:

Today I Want To:

I Will:

NIGHTLY THOUGHTS:

I Know I Am: Everyday I Get Better At:

Today I Laughed At: My Bully No Longer Affects:

Who Did I Talk To About My Bully Today? _____

My Thoughts
(Write And/Or Draw Your Thoughts)

Everything That Comes Out Of My Mouth Are Words That Uplift And Inspire.

Strong Enough

MORNING THOUGHTS:

Date: Mood:

I Woke Up Thinking:

Today I Want To:

I Will:

NIGHTLY THOUGHTS:

I Know I Am: Everyday I Get Better At:

Today I Laughed At: My Bully No Longer Affects:

Who Did I Talk To About My Bully Today? _____

My Thoughts
(Write And/Or Draw Your Thoughts)

Strong Enough

MORNING THOUGHTS:

Date: Mood:

I Woke Up Thinking:

Today I Want To:

I Will:

NIGHTLY THOUGHTS:

I Know I Am: Everyday I Get Better At:

Today I Laughed At: My Bully No Longer Affects:

Who Did I Talk To About My Bully Today? _____

My Thoughts
(Write And/Or Draw Your Thoughts)

I Will Become Everything I Said I Will Be.

Made in the USA
Columbia, SC
16 June 2019